Living Well With God

Easy read Bible lessons for people who find reading hard

By Jo Acharya

Copyright © 2023 Joanna Acharya

First published 2023 by Valley of Springs.

The right of Joanna Acharya to be identified as the author of this work has been asserted by her in accordance with the Copyright, Designs and Patents Act 1988.

All rights reserved.
No part of this publication may be reproduced, stored in a retrieval system, or transmitted in any form or by any means, electronic, mechanical, photocopying, recording or otherwise, without the prior written permission of the publisher.

ISBN 978-1-7399273-0-1

Scripture quotations are from the Holy Bible: Easy-to-Read Version™, Anglicized.
Copyright © 2013 World Bible Translation Center, a subsidiary of Bible League International.

Cover design by Leah Jeffery. Cover image and most inner images sourced from Freepik.
Images on P14 and 78 sourced from Adobe Stock. All images used with permission.

What other people are saying about 'Living Well with God'…

"Living Well With God' is a really accessible, easy to read, and easy to understand collection of Bible studies, which people of all abilities will find helpful. Based around passages from the Easy to Read Version (ERV) of the Bible, there are sessions to follow linked to topics that will meet the needs of anyone.

I love the use of simple language, helpful illustrations, as well as things to think about and fill in that make this resource really interactive. I thoroughly recommend 'Living Well With God' and encourage you to give it a try!"

Mark Arnold
Additional Needs Ministry Director, Urban Saints

'Living Well With God' is an excellent Bible resource for people who aren't natural readers to get to know the God who loves us all. Through weekly readings over one year, this easy-to-read book with graphics will help churches disciple those who find reading hard. Jo brings clarity and understanding to Bible truths in an accessible, consistent format in her mission to show God's way is the best way to live.

Tim Wood
CEO, Through The Roof charity

Contents

About this book	Page 6
How to find a Bible verse	Page 8
Learning to rest	Page 11
Loving my body	Page 21
Getting along with people	Page 31
My part in God's plan	Page 41
Understanding my feelings	Page 51
Understanding my thoughts	Page 61
God's special gift of grace	Page 71
Who God says I am	Page 81
Getting to know God	Page 91

Following Jesus	Page 101
Trusting God when life is hard	Page 111
Winning the spiritual war	Page 121
Living forever with God	Page 131
Keep learning	Page 141
About Jo	Page 142
Thanks	Page 143
Word meanings	Page 144

About this book

Hello!

My name is Jo and I wrote this book.
It is all about God's plan for living a good life.
God made us, and he loves us.
So he knows the best way to live!

In this book you will learn what the Bible says
about different parts of life.
I hope it will help you get to know God better.

This book is for people who find reading hard.
It has easy words and helpful pictures.
You can read this book on your own,
or you can ask someone to help you.

This book is an easy read version of my first book,
'Refresh: A Wellness Devotional for the Whole Christian Life'.

How to read this book

Each week you will read a part of the Bible.
And you will learn something about God's plan
for living a good life.

There are 2 questions to help you understand.
There is a prayer you can pray to God.
And there are some more questions to help you
think about your week.

There is one Bible lesson each week.
But you can read them faster or slower if you like!

There are 4 Bible lessons in each topic.
At the end of a topic you will think about what you have learned.
Then you will move on to the next topic.

If you need help

If you do not know how to look up a verse in the Bible,
you can find out on the next page.

There are some words in this book that you might not know.
They are written in red.

You can find meanings for the
red words on page 144.

It is a good idea to talk to
another Christian about what
you are learning.

They can help you if you have
questions or want to know
more.

Choosing the right Bible

There are lots of different Bibles.
They say the same things,
but they use different words.

Try to use a Bible that has easy words that you can understand. You can use a paper Bible or a Bible app on your phone.

In this book, Bible verses come from the Easy-to-Read Version (ERV). If you have a different version of the Bible, the words will be a bit different.

How to find a Bible verse

The Bible is made up of books, chapters and verses.
The chapters and verses have numbers.
This is to help you find the part of the Bible you are looking for.

In this book, Bible verses are written like this:
Ephesians chapter 3 verses 17-18.
We are going to find this part of the Bible.

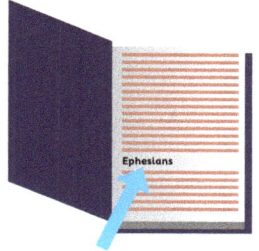
The book is Ephesians.
In the front of your Bible there is a list of all the books and the pages they start on.
Can you find the page where the book of Ephesians starts?

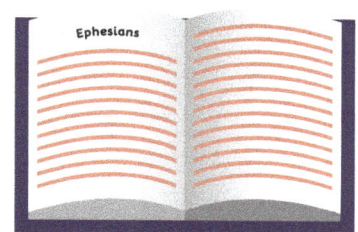

We need to find chapter 3.
Can you see the big number 1 at the start of Ephesians?
That is chapter 1.
Can you find a big number 3?
That is chapter 3.

Now we need to find verses 17-18.
Can you see the little numbers above the words in chapter 3? Those are the verses.
Can you find the little number 17?
You have found Ephesians chapter 3 verse 17!
Read verses 17 and 18.

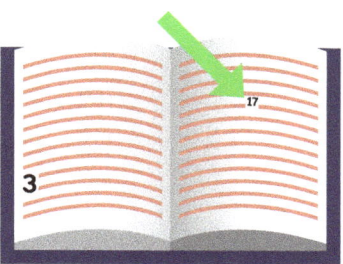

It should say something like this:

> [17] I pray that Christ will live in your hearts because of your faith. I pray that your life will be strong in love and be built on love. [18] And I pray that you and all God's holy people will have the power to understand the greatness of Christ's love—how wide, how long, how high, and how deep that love is.

Now you know how to find a Bible verse in a paper Bible.

If you have a smart phone, you can download a Bible app. In a Bible app you can read the Bible and find verses. You can make the words bigger. And some Bible apps can read the words to you.

If you need help, ask someone to show you how to use the Bible app.

Learning to rest

God does not want me
to work hard all the time.
He wants me to rest as well.
That is the best way to live.

Learning to rest: week 1

Date _____

> **The LORD worked six days and made the sky, the earth, the sea, and everything in them. And on the seventh day, he rested. In this way the LORD blessed the Sabbath— the day of rest. He made that a very special day.**
>
> **(Exodus chapter 20 verse 11)**

God's people were in a bad place.
They had to work very hard. They did not get paid.

Then God saved them! He looked after them.
He told them the best way to live.

Read Exodus chapter 20 verses 8-11

God told his people that one day in the week would be a special day. It was a day for them to rest.

On that day they spent time with God and with each other. They did not do any work at all!

They remembered that God rested too.
God rested after he made the world.

God made me. He knows the best way for me to live.
God says it is good to do work, and it is good to rest as well.

I can rest by going to sleep at night.
And I can do relaxing things
during the day.

Rest is a good gift!
God gave me this gift
because he loves me.

1. How do you like to rest?

2. What makes it hard for you to rest?

Dear Father God,

Thank you for telling me the best way to live. Please help me rest when you want me to.

Amen.

Thinking about this week

What has been good?

What has been hard?

How have I been feeling?

What am I thankful for?

How have I rested?

Who can I thank?

Learning to rest: week 2

Date _____

> **When I go to bed, I sleep in peace,
> because, Lord, you keep me safe.**
>
> **(Psalms chapter 4 verse 8)**

God chose a man called David to be the new king.
But this made the old king angry. He tried to kill David.

David ran away and hid from the king.
He wrote this psalm while he was hiding.

Read Psalms chapter 4 verses 6 -8

David trusted God even though he was afraid.
He knew God was bigger and stronger than him.

So David went to sleep. He trusted God to keep him safe.

Sometimes I think I am too busy to rest.
But that is not true.

Resting helps me remember that God is bigger and stronger than me. It helps me to trust him.

God kept David safe while he was sleeping.
I can trust God,
just like David did.
God looks after me
while I rest.

1. Do you ever think you are too busy to rest?

2. How does it feel to know that God is bigger and stronger than you?

Dear Father God,

Thank you that you are bigger and stronger than me. Please help me to trust you like David did.

Amen.

Thinking about this week

What has been good?

What has been hard?

How have I been feeling?

Do I need any help?

How have I rested?

Who can I ask for help?

Learning to rest: week 3

Date _____

> [Jesus said to his followers,] "Come with me. We will go to a quiet place to be alone. There we will get some rest."
>
> (Mark chapter 6 verse 31)

Jesus was very busy! Everyone needed his help. People kept asking him to do things, all day long! Now Jesus was tired. He needed to rest.

Read Mark chapter 6 verses 31-34 and verses 45-46

Jesus tried to take a break. But the people followed him!
So he talked to them and helped them.
Then he went away on his own to rest and pray.

It is good for me to work hard and help people.
But God knows I need to rest as well, just like Jesus.

If I get very tired it makes me feel upset.
So when I start to feel tired I know
I need to take a break.

Sometimes I need to finish
something before I can rest.
But I stop and rest
as soon as I can.
Resting is good for me!

1. How do you feel when you get tired?

2. How can you tell when you need a break?

Dear Father God,

Thank you that you worked hard and rested as well. Please help me to rest when I need to.

Amen.

Thinking about this week

What has been good?

What has been hard?

How have I been feeling?

How have I been kind?

How have I rested?

Who has been kind to me?

Learning to rest: week 4

Date _____

> [Jesus said,] "Come to me all of you who are tired from the heavy burden you have been forced to carry. I will give you rest."
> (Matthew chapter 11 verse 28)

Jesus told people to come to him if they needed a rest.
But he was not talking about rest for their bodies.
He was talking about rest for their hearts.
He can give me this rest too.

Read Matthew chapter 11 verses 28 - 30

Following Jesus does not make everything easy.
Even the people in the Bible had problems.
Some of them had very big problems!

I have problems too. But Jesus can help me. He is very strong!
He is with me even when things go wrong.

Sometimes I try to do good things to make Jesus love me.
But he already loves me!
He loves me even when I do bad things.
He never stops loving me.

Jesus said I can feel safe with him. I can talk to him when I feel worried or upset.
He will always help me.

Feeling safe with Jesus is the best kind of rest.

1. What makes you feel safe with Jesus?

2. What do you want Jesus to help you with?

Dear Lord Jesus,

Thank you that you love me.
Please help me feel safe with you.

Amen.

Thinking about this week

What has been good?	What has been hard?
How have I been feeling?	Is there anything I want to talk about?
How have I rested?	Who can I talk with?

Thinking about this topic

| What was this topic about? | What new things have I learned? |

| What has helped me? | Do I have any questions? |

| What did I like most? | Who can I ask? |

My prayer about learning to rest

Loving my body

God made my body.

He wants me to love my body and look after it well.

Loving my body: week 1

Date _____

> **I praise you because you made me in such a wonderful way. I know how amazing that was!**
>
> **(Psalms chapter 139 verse 14)**

Sometimes I wish my body looked different.
Sometimes I wish it worked better.

My body cannot always do the things I want it to do.
This makes me feel sad and angry.

Read Psalms chapter 139 verses 13 - 18

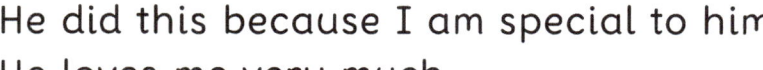

Sometimes it is hard to love my body.
But this psalm says my body was made by God.

God worked carefully to make every part of me.
He did this because I am special to him.
He loves me very much.

My body is not perfect.
But it helps me to do
so many good things.
I cannot do anything
without using my body!

When I think about the
things my body helps me
to do, I feel happy.
I can see that God made me
in a wonderful way.

God loves my body. And he wants me to love it too.

1. How do you feel about your body?

2. What are some good things your body helps you to do?

Dear Father God,
Thank you for making me.
Please help me to love my body like you do.
Amen.

Thinking about this week

What has been good?	What has been hard?
How have I been feeling?	What am I thankful for?
How have I looked after my body?	Who can I thank?

Loving my body: week 2

Date _____

> **Elijah lay down under the bush and went to sleep.
> An angel came to him and touched him.
> The angel said, "Get up and eat!"**
>
> **(1 Kings chapter 19 verse 5)**

Elijah told people how God wanted them to live.
The king did not like this. He decided to kill Elijah.
So Elijah ran away.

Read 1 Kings chapter 19 verses 3 - 8

Elijah was tired and afraid. He wanted to give up.

God loved Elijah.
He knew Elijah needed food and sleep to help him feel better.

When I feel sad or worried, there are lots of things that can help. Two things that can help are eating and sleeping. These things help my body. But they help my mind as well.

Sleep, food and exercise are important for my body and my mind. Sometimes I need medication too.
These are good gifts that God has given me. They help me look after myself well.

My body tells me when it is hungry or tired. I listen to my body and give it what it needs. This is how I look after myself well.

1. How does your body tell you what it needs?

2. What helps you when you feel sad or worried?

Dear Father God,

Thank you for food, sleep and exercise. Please help me look after myself well.

Amen.

Thinking about this week

| What has been good? | What has been hard? |

| How have I been feeling? | Do I need any help? |

| How have I looked after my body? | Who can I ask for help? |

Loving my body: week 3

Date _____

> **The Word became a man and lived among us.
> We saw his divine greatness—the greatness that
> belongs to the only Son of the Father.**
>
> **(John chapter 1 verse 14)**

God loved people so much that he did something wonderful. He came to live on earth. God lived on earth as a man called Jesus. In the Bible Jesus is sometimes called 'The Word'.

Read John chapter 1 verses 10-18

Jesus was born as a baby. He had a body like me.
He had to eat and sleep like I do.

At the end of Jesus's life on earth people hurt his body.
They nailed him to a wooden cross. This is how Jesus died.

But Jesus came back to life. And he had a wonderful new body!
God has promised that after I die,
he will give me a new body too.
Then I will live with him forever!

When my body hurts,
I remember that Jesus's body hurt too.
And I remember that I will have
a wonderful new body one day.

Jesus knows how it feels
to be a person like me.
I can ask him for help.
I know that he understands.

1. How does it feel to know that Jesus had a body like you?

2. How might your new body be different to the one you have now?

Dear Lord Jesus,

Thank you for coming to earth and living in a body like me. Please help me when my body hurts.

Amen.

Thinking about this week

What has been good?	What has been hard?
How have I been feeling?	How have I been kind??
How have I looked after my body?	Who has been kind to me?

Loving my body: week 4

Date _____

> **You should know that your body is a temple for the Holy Spirit who you received from God and who lives in you… So honour God with your body.**
>
> **(1 Corinthians chapter 6 verses 19-20)**

When Jesus lived on earth, people went to a special building to worship God. This building was called the Temple. It was God's home on earth.

But after Jesus went back to heaven, he sent the Holy Spirit to live inside every Christian. That means my body is God's new home!

Read 1 Corinthians chapter 6 verse 12-20

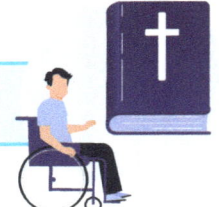

The old temple was built by very good builders.
They used gold, silver and coloured stones.
It was a very special place.

But now, the Holy Spirit lives inside everyone who follows Jesus. My body is more special to him than the most wonderful building.

My body is the home of the Holy Spirit. God wants me to keep it special.
He wants me to live in a way that makes him happy.

I try to make God happy with what I think, say and do.

1. How does it feel to know that God wants to live inside you?

2. How can you make God happy with what you think, say and do?

Dear Holy Spirit,

Thank you for deciding to live inside me. Please help me to use my body in ways that make you happy.

Amen.

Thinking about this week

What has been good?	What has been hard?
How have I been feeling?	Is there anything I want to talk about?
How have I looked after my body?	Who can I talk with?

Thinking about this topic

What was this topic about?

What new things have I learned?

What has helped me?

Do I have any questions?

What did I like most?

Who can I ask?

My prayer about loving my body

Getting along with people

Sometimes it is hard
to get along with people.
But God says we all need each other.
So God wants me to
be kind to other people.

Getting along with people: week 1

Date _____

> **Then the LORD God said,**
> **"I see that it is not good for the man to be alone. I will make the companion he needs, one just right for him."**
> **(Genesis chapter 2 verse 18)**

God made the world. Then he made the first man.
God called the man Adam.

God was happy with everything he had made.
But he was sad that Adam was alone.

Read Genesis chapter 2 verses 18-24

God made a woman called Eve.
That made Adam very happy.
Now there were two people!
Adam was not alone any more.

God wants people to help each other and have fun together.
So he made us all different. He made us good at different things.

That means I need other people.
And it means other people need me too.

It is hard for me to get along with people all the time.
There are some people I do not like.
It can even be hard to get along with people I love.

But God wants me to be kind to the people I know.
Knowing other people is better than being alone.

1. What makes it hard to get along with people?

2. Who are some of the special people in your life?

Dear Holy Spirit,

Thank you that you made us all different. Please help me to get along with the people I know.

Amen.

Thinking about this week

What has been good?	What has been hard?
How have I been feeling?	What am I thankful for?
How have I got along with people?	Who can I thank?

Getting along with people: week 2

Date _____

> **God has chosen you and made you his holy people. He loves you. So your new life should be like this: Show mercy to others. Be kind, humble, gentle and patient.**
>
> **(Colossians chapter 3 verse 12)**

Paul helped people to follow Jesus.
He wrote this letter to a group of Christians.
He told them to love each other.
He told them to be kind and caring.

Read Colossians chapter 3 verses 12-15

God wants me to be kind and caring too.
It is easy to be kind when people are kind to me.
But sometimes people upset me.
Sometimes I upset other people too.
We all do bad things sometimes.

The Holy Spirit lives inside me.
He helps me to do what God wants, even when it is hard.

When someone upsets me,
it is okay to tell them.
It is loving to give them a
chance to say sorry.
And it is good to say sorry when
I do bad things too.

God wants us all to say sorry
and forgive each other.
This is a way we can help each
other to do what God wants.

1. Is it easy for you to be kind and caring?

2. Have you ever had to say sorry or forgive someone?

Dear Father God,

Thank you that you want us to love each other. Please help me to be kind and caring to other people.

Amen.

Thinking about this week

What has been good?	What has been hard?
How have I been feeling?	Do I need any help?
How have I got along with people?	Who can I ask for help?

Getting along with people: week 3

Date _____

> **Ruth said, "Don't force me to leave you... Wherever you go, I will go. Wherever you sleep, I will sleep. Your people will be my people. Your God will be my God."**
>
> **(Ruth chapter 1 verse 16)**

Naomi was very sad.
Her husband and sons had died.
She wanted to be left alone.

Read Ruth chapter 1 verses 15-18

Ruth knew that Naomi needed a friend.
She decided to be a good friend to Naomi.
Ruth looked after Naomi until she felt better.

When someone I love is sad, it upsets me too. I want to help.
But I cannot always make them feel better.

When someone I love is sad, I try to be kind and caring.
I tell them I love them. And I pray for God to help them.
These are all ways I can be a good friend.

Sometimes I feel sad, like Naomi.
I want to be left alone.
But it is better to tell someone how I am feeling.
It is good to ask people for help.
I need good friends too.

Sometimes I help people.
Sometimes people help me.
That is the way
God wants it to be!

1. Have you ever been a good friend to someone? What happened?

2. Has someone been a good friend to you? What happened?

Dear Father God,

Thank you that I can help other people.
Thank you that other people can help me too.
Please help me to be a good friend.

Amen.

Thinking about this week

What has been good?	What has been hard?
How have I been feeling?	How have I been kind?
How have I got along with people?	Who has been kind to me?

Getting along with people: week 4

Date _____

> **You are his chosen people, the King's priests. You are a holy nation, people who belong to God... In the past you were not a special people, but now you are God's people.**
>
> **(1 Peter chapter 2 verses 9-10)**

Loving other people can be hard.
It is hard even for Christians! We are all different.
We like different things. We do not always agree.

But there is one big thing that is the same for all Christians. We are all following Jesus. The Bible says we are brothers and sisters in God's family.

Read: 1 Peter chapter 2 verses 9-12

It is hard to follow Jesus on my own.
That is why it is good to go to church.

At church I learn about God with other Christians.
We sing songs to God together. And we pray for each other.

God wants Christians to be good brothers and sisters to each other. We try to love each other.
We try to be kind and caring.
We say sorry and forgive each other.

Christians help each other to keep following Jesus. That is what God's family is all about.

1. What is good about going to church?

2. How do other Christians help you to keep following Jesus?

Dear Father God,

Thank you that I am part of your family. Please help me to be a good brother or sister to other Christians.

Amen.

Thinking about this week

What has been good?	What has been hard?
How have I been feeling?	Is there anything I want to talk about?
How have I got along with people?	Who can I talk with?

Thinking about this topic

What was this topic about?

What new things have I learned?

What has helped me?

Do I have any questions?

What did I like most?

Who can I ask?

My prayer about getting along with people

My part in God's plan

God has a good plan to make the world better.

And he wants me to be part of it!

I can work with God to make the world better.

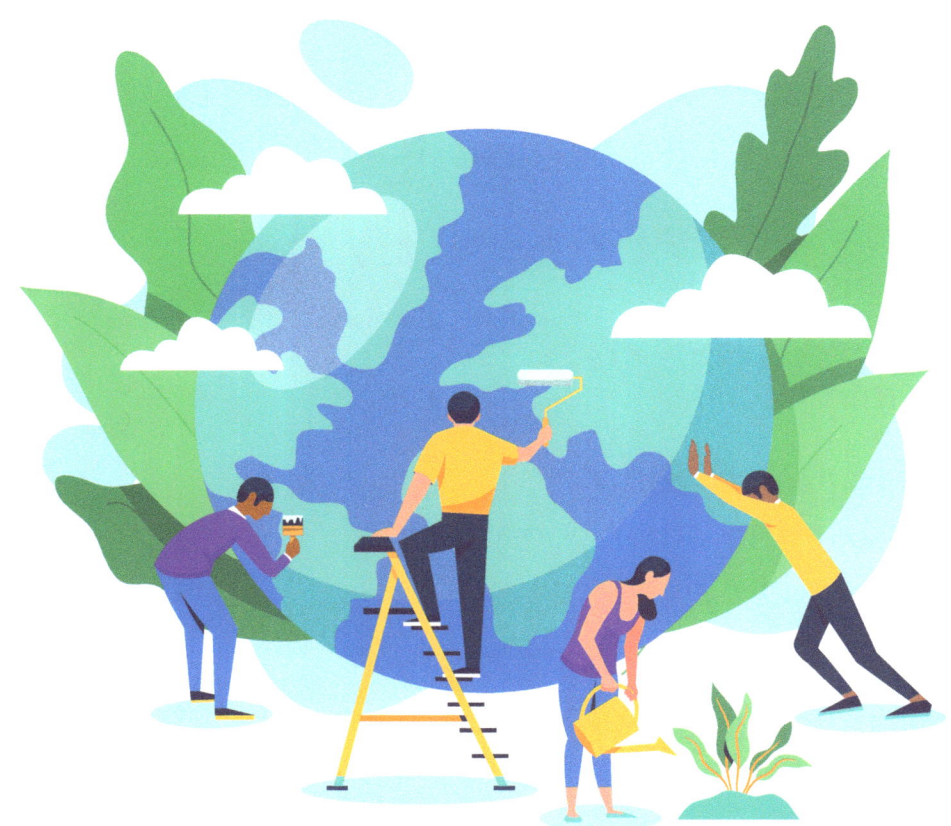

My part in God's plan: week 1

Date _____

> **All of you together are the body of Christ.
> Each one of you is a part of that body.
> (1 Corinthians chapter 12 verse 27)**

My body has lots of different parts.
They all do different things. But they are all important.

The Bible says that Christians are like Jesus's body.
Jesus is like the head. He tells us what we should do.
And we work together to do what he wants.

Read 1 Corinthians chapter 12 verses 19-27

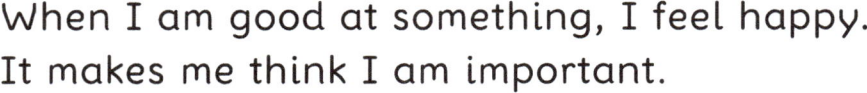

When I am good at something, I feel happy.
It makes me think I am important.

When I am not good at something, I feel sad.
It makes me think I am not important.

But the Bible says we are
all important to God.
He has made us good at
different things.

God does not want me to
compare myself to other people.
He wants me to be happy with
the way he made me.

It is good that God made us
all different. We can all work
together, like a body does.

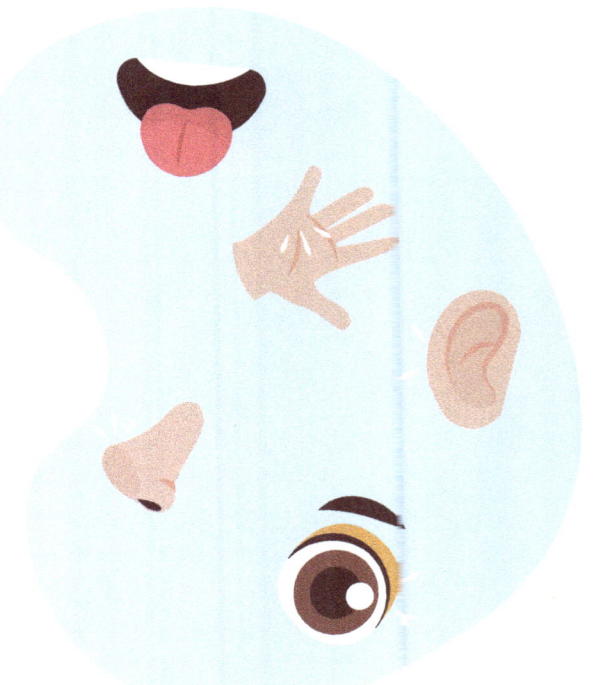

1. Have you ever compared yourself with other people? How did it make you feel?

2. What are some good things about the way God made you?

Dear Father God,

Thank you for making us all different. Please help me to be happy with the way you made me.

Amen.

Thinking about this week

| What has been good? | What has been hard? |

| How have I been feeling? | What am I thankful for? |

| How have I worked with God to make the world better? | Who can I thank? |

My part in God's plan: week 2

Date _____

> [Mordecai said to Esther,] "And who knows, maybe you have been chosen to be the queen for such a time as this."
>
> (Esther chapter 4 verse 14)

God's people were in trouble.
The king had decided to kill them all.
But there was something the king did not know.
His wife Esther was one of God's people!

Esther was afraid to talk to the king.
She thought he might kill her too!

Read: Esther chapter 4 verses 10-16

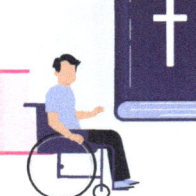

Esther trusted God. She knew what he wanted her to do.
She asked him for help.

Esther talked to the king. And the king changed his mind!
Esther became part of God's good plan.
Together, they saved the people.

Sometimes it is hard for me to trust God.
Sometimes I feel worried and afraid, like Esther.
But I know I can ask God for help.
He is always with me.

God wants me to be part of his plan.
When I trust him, he brings good things out of every part of my life.
This is how I can work with God to make the world better.

1. When is it hard for you to trust God?

2. How can you work with God to make the world better?

Dear Father God,

Thank you that you want me to be part of your good plan. Please help me to trust you.

Amen.

Thinking about this week

What has been good?	What has been hard?
How have I been feeling?	Do I need any help?
How have I worked with God to make the world better?	Who can I ask for help?

My part in God's plan: week 3

Date _____

> **I learned that the best thing for people to do is to be happy and enjoy themselves as long as they live. God wants everyone to eat, drink, and enjoy their work. These are gifts from God.**
>
> **(Ecclesiastes chapter 3 verses 12-13)**

Sometimes I think God only cares about what I do at church. But the Bible says God cares about all the things I do.

I do lots of different things in my life. God has given me lots of things to enjoy.

Read: Ecclesiastes chapter 3 verses 9-13

In church I sing songs to worship God.
But I worship him in the rest of my life too.

I ask God to be with me every day.
I talk to him while I am doing things.
I thank him for good things he has given me.
And I try to live my life in a way that makes him happy.

God wants to be part of my life every day.
I can enjoy the things he has given me.
And I can worship him in all the things I do.

That makes me happy,
and it makes God happy too!

1. What are some things you like to do?

2. How can you worship God in all the things you do?

Dear Father God,

Thank you that you want to be part of my life. Please help me to worship you in all the things I do.

Amen.

Thinking about this week

What has been good?	What has been hard?
How have I been feeling?	How have I been kind?
How have I worked with God to make the world better?	Who has been kind to me?

My part in God's plan: week 4

Date _____

> [King David prayed,] "All these things didn't come from me and my people. All these things come from you. We are only giving back to you things that came from you."'
>
> (1 Chronicles chapter 29 verse 14)

King David wanted to build a wonderful temple, where people could worship God. But God said no. He wanted David's son Solomon to build the temple instead.

So David asked all God's people to give Solomon money. The money would help Solomon build the temple.

Read: 1 Chronicles chapter 29 verses 9-16

God's people gave Solomon lots of money! David was very happy.

But David knew that God had given the people everything they had. They were really giving God's money back to God!

God gave me everything I have.
He wants me to do good things with my time and money.

Sometimes I give money to my church, or to people who need help. I use some of my time to worship God and help people.

David trusted God.
He did what God wanted instead of what he wanted.
I try to do what God wants too.
God helps me to do good things with my time and money.

1. What good things do you do with your time and money?

2. God said no to David. Has God ever said no to something you wanted?

Dear Father God,

Thank you for giving me everything I have. Please help me to do good things with my time and money.

Amen.

Thinking about this week

What has been good?	What has been hard?
How have I been feeling?	Is there anything I want to talk about?
How have I worked with God to make the world better?	Who can I talk with?

Thinking about this topic

| What was this topic about? | What new things have I learned? |

| What has helped me? | Do I have any questions? |

| What did I like most? | Who can I ask? |

My prayer about my part in God's plan

Understanding my feelings

Everyone has feelings.

My feelings are a good part of me.

God wants me to use my feelings well.

Understanding my feelings: week 1

Date _____

> **Jesus cried. And the Jews said,
> "Look! He loved Lazarus very much!"
> (John chapter 11 verses 35-36)**

Jesus had a good friend called Lazarus.
When Lazarus died, Jesus was very sad. It made him cry.

Read John chapter 11 verses 32-36

This story had a happy ending.
Jesus brought Lazarus back to life! Then he was happy again.

The Bible says that God has feelings.
He knows what it is like to feel happy, sad and angry

When God made me, he gave me feelings.
This is one of the ways I am like him!

My feelings tell me what is happening in my heart.
So it is good to think about the way I am feeling.
It helps me understand why I am feeling that way.

Sometimes I do not like my feelings.
And sometimes they are confusing.
I talk about those feelings with someone
who can help me understand them.

Understanding my feelings
helps me make good choices
about what to do next.
This is what it means to
use my feelings well.

1. When have you felt happy, sad or angry?

2. What helps you to understand your feelings?

Dear Father God,

Thank you that you have feelings just like me. Please help me understand my feelings and use them well.

Amen.

Thinking about this week

What has been good?	What has been hard?
How have I been feeling?	What am I thankful for?
What has helped me understand my feelings?	Who can I thank?

Understanding my feelings: week 2

Date _____

> **Trust the LORD completely,
> and don't depend on your own knowledge.
> (Proverbs chapter 3 verse 5)**

Sometimes my feelings make me believe things that are not true.
So I cannot always trust my feelings.
But I can always trust God.

Read Proverbs chapter 3 verses 5-8

Feeling upset might make me believe nobody loves me.
Feeling angry might make me believe I am right and everyone else is wrong.

If my feelings make me believe things that are not true,
I can get hurt. And I can hurt other people.

Some kinds of feelings need help from a doctor.
If I feel sad or worried all the time,
it is important to tell someone.

This is why thinking about my feelings is helpful.
Understanding my feelings helps me work out what is true.
I can also read the Bible to see if my feelings
agree with what God says.

God wants to help me
know the truth.
It is good to trust God more
than I trust my feelings.

1. Have your feelings ever made you believe something that was not true? What happened?

2. How can you work out what is true?

Dear Father God,

Thank you that you know what is true. Please help me to trust you more than I trust my feelings.

Amen.

Thinking about this week

What has been good?	What has been hard?
How have I been feeling?	Do I need any help?
What has helped me understand my feelings?	Who can I ask for help?

Understanding my feelings: week 3

Date _____

> My God, my God, why have you left me?
> You seem too far away to save me,
> too far to hear my cries for help!
> (Psalms chapter 22 verse 1)

Psalms is a book of songs. Some are happy, some are angry and some are sad. People sang these songs to God to tell him how they were feeling.

This song was written by King David.

Read Psalms chapter 22 verses 1-5

When David started his song he felt very sad.
But then he thought about how God had helped people in the past. David knew that he could trust God to help him too.

At the end of the song, David was happy.
He thanked God for listening to him and helping him.

God loves me. And he knows that my life is hard sometimes. God wants me to talk to him about my feelings.

I can talk to God even when I am sad or angry. He helps me remember the good things in my life. He helps me to trust him. Talking to God helps me feel better.

1. How does David's song make you feel?

2. Can you think of a time when talking to God helped you feel better?

Dear Father God,

Thank you that I can talk to you about my feelings. Please help me when I feel sad or angry.

Amen.

Thinking about this week

| What has been good? | What has been hard? |

| How have I been feeling? | How have I been kind? |

| What has helped me understand my feelings | Who has been kind to me? |

Understanding my feelings: week 4

Date _____

> **Always be full of joy. Never stop praying.
> Whatever happens, always be thankful.
> This is how God wants you to live in Christ Jesus.
> (1 Thessalonians chapter 5 verses 16-18)**

The Bible says that all the good things I have are gifts from God.
God has given me lots of good things.
He loves it when I say thank you to him.

Read 1 Thessalonians chapter 5 verses 12-18

Sometimes my life is hard.
Then I forget all the good things I have.
I do not feel like saying thank you to God.

But when I thank God for the good things, it helps me feel better.
It does not make me forget the things that are hard.
But it helps me remember the good things too.

When I try, I can find lots of things to say thank you for!
So I thank God for 3 things every night before I go to bed.
I write them down and read them again when I feel sad.

Saying thank you to God makes me happy.
And it makes him happy too!

1. Has anyone ever thanked you for a gift you gave them? How did it make you feel?

2. Can you think of 3 things to thank God for?

Dear Father God,

Thank you for all the good things you have given me. Please help me to remember them when I feel sad.

Amen.

Thinking about this week

| What has been good? | What has been hard? |

| How have I been feeling? | Is there anything I want to talk about? |

| What has helped me understand my feelings? | Who can I talk with? |

Thinking about this topic

What was this topic about?

What new things have I learned?

What has helped me?

Do I have any questions?

What did I like most?

Who can I ask?

My prayer about understanding my feelings

Understanding my thoughts

What I think about is very important. God wants to help me think thoughts that are good and true.

Understanding my thoughts: week 1

Date _____

> **We also capture every thought
> and make it give up and obey Christ.**
>
> **(2 Corinthians chapter 10 verse 5)**

My mind is very clever.
It remembers the things that happen to me.
And it fits them all together.
This helps me to understand the world.

But sometimes my mind gets things wrong.
This makes me think thoughts that are not true.

Read 2 Corinthians chapter 10 verses 3-5

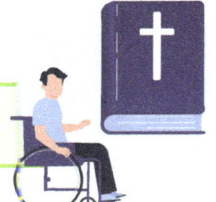

Some thoughts help me. But some thoughts hurt me.

Sometimes I think God loves me. This is good and true!
This thought helps me.
But sometimes I think I am stupid.
This is not true! This thought hurts me.

I do not always know if my thoughts are good and true.
So I write them down.
Then I talk about them with someone I trust.
I also ask God to help me work out
if my thoughts are good and true.

God helps me say yes
to thoughts that help me.
And he helps me say no
to thoughts that hurt me.

1. What might happen if you think thoughts that are not true?

2. Write down some of your thoughts. Are they good and true? Do they help you or hurt you?

Dear Father God,

Thank you for my mind. Please help me work out if my thoughts are good and true.

Amen.

Thinking about this week

What has been good?	What has been hard?
How have I been feeling?	What am I thankful for?
What good thoughts are in my mind?	Who can I thank?

Understanding my thoughts: week 2

Date _____

> "To fear and respect the Lord is wisdom.
> To turn away from evil is understanding."
> (Job chapter 28 verse 28)

It is important to know the truth.
Knowing the truth helps me to make good choices.
But sometimes it is hard to work out what is true.

Read Job chapter 28 verses 23-28

God always knows the truth.
As I get to know God, he teaches me the best way to live.
He helps me work out what is true and what is not.
He helps me make good choices.

One way to get to know God is to read the Bible.
The Bible is a special book.
It was written by people who knew God very well.
The Holy Spirit helped them to say what he wanted them to say.

When I read the Bible, the Holy Spirit
talks to me in my mind.
He helps me to understand
what I am reading.
He helps me to know God better.
And he helps me to work out
what is true.

1. How can knowing the truth help you to make good choices?

2. Can you think of something the Bible says about God?

Dear Holy Spirit,

Thank you that you helped the people who wrote the Bible. Please help me to know you better. Please help me to work out what is true.

Amen.

Thinking about this week

What has been good?	What has been hard?
How have I been feeling?	Do I need any help?
What good thoughts are in my mind?	Who can I ask for help?

Understanding my thoughts: week 3

Date _____

> **Brothers and sisters, continue to think about what is good and worthy of praise. Think about what is true and honourable and right and pure and beautiful and respected.**
>
> **(Philippians chapter 4 verse 8)**

Paul was in prison because he followed Jesus.
He wrote this letter to a group of Christians.

Read Philippians chapter 4 verses 4-9

Some things in Paul's life were very hard.
But he did not want to think about hard things all the time.
He wanted to think about good things too.
This helped him to keep going.

Some things in my life are hard.
I need to think about these things sometimes.
But if I think about hard things all the time, I feel sad and worried.
This makes me want to give up.

So I try to think about the good things in my life too.
When I think about good things, it helps me feel better.
It helps me to keep going.

Sometimes it is hard to think about good things.
So I ask someone I trust to help me.
And I ask God to help me too.

1. What good things do you like to think about?

2. How can thinking about good things help you to keep going?

Dear Father God,

Thank you for all the good things in my life. Please help me to think about good things as well as hard things.

Amen.

Thinking about this week

| What has been good? | What has been hard? |

| How have I been feeling? | How have I been kind? |

| What good thoughts are in my mind? | Who has been kind to me? |

Understanding my thoughts: week 4

Date _____

> I ask only one thing from the LORD.
> This is what I want most:
> Let me live in the LORD's house all my life,
> enjoying the LORD's beauty.
>
> (Psalms chapter 27 verse 4)

King David wrote this psalm.
He was thinking about how wonderful God is.
There were lots of things going on in David's life.
Some were very hard things.
But thinking about God always made David feel happy.

Read Psalms chapter 27 verses 1-4

There are lots of things going on in my life.
Some are good things. Some are hard things.
Thinking about all these things fills up my mind.
Sometimes that makes me forget about God.

But I do not want to forget about God. So I spend time thinking about what he is like. I think about how strong God is.
I think about all the ways he helps me.
And I think about how much he loves me.

God has promised that Christians will live with him forever.
This is a wonderful thing to think about!

Even when my life is hard, thinking about God makes me feel happy.

1. How might the things in your life make you forget about God?

2. What are some thoughts about God that make you happy?

Dear Father God,

Thank you that you are so wonderful and good. Please help me to think about you every day.

Amen.

Thinking about this week

What has been good?	What has been hard?
How have I been feeling?	Is there anything I want to talk about?
What good thoughts are in my mind?	Who can I talk with?

Thinking about this topic

| What was this topic about? | What new things have I learned? |

| What has helped me? | Do I have any questions? |

| What did I like most? | Who can I ask? |

My prayer about understanding my thoughts

God's special gift of grace

I do not have to work hard to make God love me.

He already loves me!

He has given me a special gift.

It is called grace.

God's special gift of grace: week 1

Date _____

> **I want to do what is good, but I don't do it.**
> **I don't do the good that I want to do.**
> **I do the evil that I don't want to do.**
> **(Romans chapter 7 verses 18-19)**

Before Paul met Jesus, he tried very hard to do good things.
But he could not stop doing bad things.
This made him very sad.

Read Romans chapter 7 verses 18-25

I really want to do good things.
But I feel like something inside me wants to do bad things.
That is how Paul felt too. He said that thing inside us is called sin.

God knows we cannot stop doing bad things.
Sin is stronger than we are. We cannot beat sin on our own.
That is why Father God sent Jesus to save us from sin.

Jesus is much stronger than sin.
When he died on the cross, he beat sin forever.
He took away all the bad things we have done.
It is like they were never there!

I still do bad things sometimes.
But I know Jesus has already taken those bad things away.
So I say sorry to God,
and he forgives me.
God never stops loving me.

1. What does it mean to say sorry to God?

2. How does it feel when God forgives you?

Dear Father God,

I am sorry for the bad things I have done. Thank you for sending Jesus to take those bad things away. Please forgive me.

Amen.

Thinking about this week

What has been good?	What has been hard?
How have I been feeling?	What am I thankful for?
What good things has God done for me?	Who can I thank?

God's special gift of grace: week 2

Date _____

> You have been saved by grace because you believed.
> You did not save yourselves; it was a gift from God.
> You are not saved by the things you have done,
> so there is nothing to boast about.
>
> (Ephesians chapter 2 verses 8-9)

Sometimes I believe I am a good person.
I think God will love me because I do good things.

Sometimes I believe I am a bad person.
I think God will stop loving me because I do bad things.

Read Ephesians chapter 2 verses 1-10

God loves me because he wants to love me!
It is not because of anything I do.
It is because he made me to be his friend.

Sin makes me do bad things. It makes me turn away from God.
It hurts me. It hurts other people too.
I cannot beat sin. I need help.
So Father God sent Jesus to save me from sin.

Jesus took away the bad things I have done.
He saved me from sin.
And he beat sin forever!

I did not work to save myself.
God saved me because he loves me.
This is his special gift of grace.
Now I can be his friend.
Being friends with God is very good!

1. What is special about God's grace?

2. How does it feel to know that God wants to be friends with you?

Dear Father God,

Thank you for giving me your grace. Thank you that I can be your friend.

Amen

Thinking about this week

What has been good?

What has been hard?

How have I been feeling?

Do I need help?

What good things has God done for me?

Who can I ask for help?

God's special gift of grace: week 3

Date _____

> We have freedom now, because Christ made us free.
> So stand strong in that freedom.
> Don't go back into slavery again.
>
> (Galatians chapter 5 verse 1)

Paul was very upset.
Some people were telling Christians to follow lots of rules.
They said Christians had to work hard to be friends with God.

Paul wrote a letter to the Christians.
He said those people were wrong.

Read Galatians chapter 5 verses 1-6

God's rules are good.
But nobody can follow all the rules.
We cannot be good all the time.
That is why God gave us grace instead.

God's grace is better than rules, because it is a gift.
We do not have to work to get God's grace.
All we need to do is say thank you!

I do not have to work hard to make God love me.
He already loves me!
That makes me happy.

I love God too.
So I want to make him happy.
I try to do what God wants.
I know that is the best way to live.

1. Why is grace better than rules?

2. Why is it good to do what God wants?

Dear Father God,

Thank you that I do not have to work to make you love me. I love you too. Please help me to make you happy.

Amen.

Thinking about this week

| What has been good? | What has been hard? |

| How have I been feeling? | How have I been kind? |

| What good things has God done for me? | Who has been kind to me? |

God's special gift of grace: week 4

Date _____

> [God said to Jonah,] "If you can get upset over a plant, surely I can feel sorry for a big city like Nineveh… There are more than 120,000 people there who did not know they were doing wrong."
>
> (Jonah chapter 4 verse 11)

The people in Nineveh were doing lots of bad things. This made God angry. He sent Jonah to tell them to stop doing bad things.

The people listened to Jonah. They were very sorry for what they had done. God decided to forgive them.

This made Jonah very angry! He thought God should punish the people. He did not want God to forgive them.

Read Jonah chapter 4 verses 1-11

When someone upsets me, I want God to punish them.
I do not want God to forgive them.

But I know that I do bad things too. God forgave me.
He gave me his grace. He wants to forgive other people too.
He wants to give grace to everyone!

God always loves me and forgives me.
That makes me feel happy.
It makes me want to love
and forgive other people.
So I ask God to give grace
to people who upset me.

1. Have you ever felt angry like Jonah?

2. Who can you ask God to give grace to?

Dear Father God,

Thank you that you want to give grace to everyone. Please help me to forgive people who upset me. Please help me to love them like you love them.

Amen.

Thinking about this week

What has been good?	What has been hard?
How have I been feeling?	Is there anything I want to talk about?
What good things has God done for me?	Who can I talk to?

Thinking about this topic

| What was this topic about? | What new things have I learned? |

| What has helped me? | Do I have any questions? |

| What did I like most? | Who can I ask? |

My prayer about God's special gift of grace

Who God says I am

The Bible says God made me.
He loves me just as I am.
And he is helping me grow into
the person he made me to be!

Who God says I am: week 1

Date _____

> **And before the world was made, God decided to make us his own children through Jesus Christ. This was what God wanted, and it pleased him to do it.**
>
> **(Ephesians chapter 1 verse 5)**

Lots of different things make me who I am.
Some are things I like and things I am good at.
Some are places I go and people I love.

All these things are important to me.
But they do not stay the same forever.
Things in my life keep changing. And I change too!

There is only one thing about me that stays the same forever.
I am God's special child! That will never change.

Read Ephesians chapter 1 verses 3-6

Father God made me. He is my father in heaven.
And he chose me to be his child before he made the world!
This is wonderful. It is the most important part of who I am.

I am God's special child.
He loves me very much.
And he is always with me.
These things are true forever.
Even if everything else changes,
God will still love me.
Whatever happens,
I will always be God's child.

1. What are some things that make you who you are? Have they changed?

2. What is good about being God's child?

Dear Father God,

Thank you that you chose me to be your child. Thank you that your love for me never changes. Please help me remember these things.

Amen.

Thinking about this week

What has been good?	What has been hard?

How have I been feeling?	What am I thankful for?

When have I felt God's love for me?	Who can I thank?

Who God says I am: week 2

Date _____

> **When anyone is in Christ, it is a whole new world.
> The old things are gone; suddenly, everything is new!**
> **(2 Corinthians chapter 5 verse 17)**

Something happened when I decided to follow Jesus.
The Holy Spirit came to live inside me.
That was a very big change!

Read 2 Corinthians chapter 5 verses 16-19

Being a Christian is not just about following rules.
God knows that nobody can follow all the rules.
That is why he sent Jesus to take away the bad things we have done. Then he gave us his grace!

But now the Holy Spirit lives inside me. He helps me.
He is changing my heart and making me strong inside.
Now it is easier for me to do what God wants.
And it is easier to say no to the bad things I used to do.

I am happy because God is changing me.
I am still me.
But I am different too.
I am growing into the person
God made me to be.
That is the best me I can be!

1. How have you changed since you started following Jesus?

2. Can you think of a time when the Holy Spirit helped you do what God wanted?

Dear Holy Spirit,

Thank you that you are changing me. Please help me to do what you want. Please help me grow into the person you made me to be.

Amen.

Thinking about this week

What has been good?	What has been hard?
How have I been feeling?	Do I need any help?
When have I felt God's love for me?	Who can I ask for help?

Who God says I am: week 3

Date _____

> [Jesus said,] "But the Holy Spirit will come on you and give you power. You will be my witnesses. You will tell people everywhere about me."
>
> (Acts chapter 1 verse 8)

It was time for Jesus to go back to heaven.
He gave his followers an important job to do.
He told them to tell everyone about the things he had done.
But Jesus's followers were afraid!

Then Jesus sent the Holy Spirit to live inside his followers.
The Holy Spirit made them strong inside.
He helped them to tell people about Jesus.

Read Acts chapter 1 verses 6-11

Jesus wants everyone to know about him.
That is what I want too.
But sometimes I am afraid to tell people about him.

So I show people what Jesus is like by doing what God wants.
And when people ask me why I love God,
I ask the Holy Spirit for help. He makes me strong inside.
He helps me talk about all the ways God helps me.

I want everyone to know
how much God loves them.
I want everyone to be
friends with him.

1. When you do what God wants, how does this show people what Jesus is like?

2. If someone asked you why you love God, what would you say?

Dear Holy Spirit,

Thank you that you make me strong inside when I am afraid. Please help me to tell people about Jesus. Please help everyone to be friends with God.

Amen

Thinking about this week

What has been good?

What has been hard?

How have I been feeling?

How have I been kind?

When have I felt God's love for me?

Who has been kind to me?

Who God says I am: week 4

Date _____

> **I am sure that the good work God began in you will continue until he completes it on the day when Jesus Christ comes again.**
>
> **(Philippians chapter 1 verse 6)**

Even though I am a Christian, I still do bad things.
And sometimes I say or do things that hurt other people.

But the Holy Spirit is changing my heart.
I am getting better at being kind and caring.
And I make better choices than I used to.

God is helping me grow into the person he made me to be.
He will never give up on me.

Read Philippians chapter 1 verses 3-6

When I do something bad,
I try not to get angry with myself.
I say sorry to God.
And I say sorry to the people I have hurt.
Then I keep on trying to do what God wants.

God always forgives me. He gives me his grace.
And he keeps helping me to live
in a way that makes him happy.

God will never give up on me.
So I will not give up on myself either!

1. How are you getting better at making good choices?

2. When you do something bad, what helps you to not give up on yourself?

Dear Father God,

Thank you that you forgive me when I do bad things. Thank you that you never give up on me. Please help me not to give up on myself either.

Amen.

Thinking about this week

What has been good?	What has been hard?
How have I been feeling?	Is there anything I want to talk about?
When have I felt God's love for me?	Who can I talk with?

Thinking about this topic

| What was this topic about? | What new things have I learned? |

| What has helped me? | Do I have any questions? |

| What did I like most? | Who can I ask? |

My prayer about who God says I am

Getting to know God

God wants me to be his friend.
Spending time with God helps me
get to know him better.
It helps our friendship to grow.

Getting to know God: week 1

Date _____

> LORD, help me learn your ways.
> Show me how you want me to live.
> Guide me and teach me your truths.
> You are my God, my Saviour.
>
> (Psalms chapter 25 verses 4-5)

God wants me to be his friend.
That is the reason he made me!
So I want to learn more about what God is like.
I want to get to know him better.

Read Psalms chapter 25 verses 4-10

God is with me all the time.
He is with me when I wake up and when I go to bed.
He is even with me when I am busy doing things.

So I can talk to God any time.
I can pray out loud, or quietly in my mind.
He is always listening.

It is important to have special time with God too.
In my special time with God,
I think about how great he is.
I worship him and pray.
I read the Bible and listen to him.
I ask him to show me
the best way to live.

God loves it when I
spend time with him.

1. What do you do in your special time with God?

2. What do you want to say to God today?

Dear Father God,

Thank you that you love spending time with me. Please help me to have special time with you. Please help me get to know you better.

Amen.

Thinking about this week

What has been good?	What has been hard?
How have I been feeling?	What am I thankful for?
How have I spent time with God?	Who can I thank?

Getting to know God: week 2

Date _____

> **Your words are so sweet to me,
> like the taste of honey!**
>
> **(Psalms chapter 119 verse 103)**

The Bible was written by people who knew God very well.
So reading the Bible helps me get to know God too.

The Bible tells me what God is like.
And it teaches me the best way to live.

Read Psalms chapter 119 verses 97-104

The Holy Spirit helped the people who wrote the Bible.
He gave them thoughts and ideas.
He helped them to say what he wanted them to say.
So the Bible is also a message to people from God.

Reading the Bible is like having a talk with God.
The Holy Spirit talks to me through the words in the Bible.
And I can talk to him about what I am reading.
The Holy Spirit helps me hear what God wants to say to me.

It is not always easy to read the Bible.
Sometimes I need help to understand it.
So I talk to another Christian
who knows God well.
They can help me
understand the Bible.

1. Who helps you to understand the Bible?

2. Which parts of the Bible do you like best?

Dear Holy Spirit,

Thank you for the Bible. Please help me to read the Bible and understand it. Please help me hear what you want to say to me.

Amen.

Thinking about this week

| What has been good? | What has been hard? |

| How have I been feeling? | Do I need any help? |

| How have I spent time with God? | Who can I ask for help? |

Getting to know God: week 3

Date _____

> [Jesus prayed,] "Our Father in heaven,
> we pray that your name will always be kept holy.
> We pray that your kingdom will come—
> that what you want will be done here on earth,
> the same as in heaven."
>
> (Matthew chapter 6 verses 9-10)

Jesus's followers asked him how to pray.
So Jesus taught them this prayer.
If I do not know what to say to God, I pray this prayer.
Sometimes I change the words to make it about my life.

Read Matthew chapter 6 verses 6-13

When I pray, I tell God how much I love him.
I ask him to make the world better.
I ask him to give me the things I need.
I say sorry for the bad things I have done.
And I ask him to look after everyone.

I say all kinds of prayers to God.
Praying reminds me that God is bigger and stronger than I am.

Sometimes I think God is saying
something to me in my mind.
I want to make sure it is not
just my own thoughts.
So I talk to another Christian
who knows God well.
They can help me understand
what God is saying to me.

1. What kinds of prayers do you say to God?

2. How can you know if God is saying something to you?

Dear Father God,

Thank you that I can talk to you any time. Please help me say all kinds of prayers to you. Please help me understand what you are saying to me.

Amen.

Thinking about this week

What has been good?	What has been hard?
How have I been feeling?	How have I been kind?
How have I spent time with God?	Who has been kind to me?

Getting to know God: week 4

Date _____

> **We should... encourage each other to show love and do good works. We must not quit meeting together, as some are doing. No, we need to keep on encouraging each other.**
> **(Hebrews chapter 10 verses 24-25)**

It is very hard to follow Jesus on my own.
I need help from other people. And they need my help too!

The Bible says it is good to spend time with other Christians.
We can pray and worship God together.
And we can help each other when life is hard.

Read Hebrews chapter 10 verses 19-25

Everyone is different.
And everyone has a different friendship with God.
So I can learn more about God from other people.
And they can learn more about God from me.
We can all help each other understand new things about God.

This is why I go to church.
Worshipping God with other Christians
is another way I get to know him better.

God loves it when Christians
worship him together.
He loves it when we
learn from each other.
And he loves it when we
help each other
to keep following Jesus.

1. What is your friendship with God like?

2. What is something you have learned about God? Maybe you can tell someone else about this!

Dear Father God,

Thank you for the other Christians I know. Please help us to help each other. Please help us to follow Jesus together.

Amen

Thinking about this week

What has been good?	What has been hard?
How have I been feeling?	Is there anything I want to talk about?
How have I spent time with God?	Who can I talk with?

Thinking about this topic

| What was this topic about? | What new things have I learned? |

| What has helped me? | Do I have any questions? |

| What did I like most? | Who can I ask? |

My prayer about getting to know God

Following Jesus

I want to be more like Jesus.
So I try to live the way he lived.
This is what it means to
follow Jesus in my life.

Following Jesus: week 1

Date _____

> Human, the LORD has told you what goodness is.
> This is what he wants from you:
> be fair to other people, love kindness and loyalty,
> and humbly obey your God.
>
> (Micah chapter 6 verse 8)

The Bible says that God is always good.
He loves all the people he made. So I want God to be my king.
That means I want to live in a way that makes him happy.

Read Micah chapter 6 verses 6-8

Sometimes I do not want to do what God says.
Sometimes I want to do things God says are bad.

But then I remember how good God is.
I remember that he is my king.
I know God always leads me the right way.
So I try to do what he says, even when I do not want to.

God is a good king.
He wants me to do good things.
He wants me to be kind and caring.
He wants me to be honest and fair.

God knows me even better
than I know myself.
So I can trust him to show me
the best way to live.

1. What does it mean for God to be your king?

2. How does God want people to live?

Dear Father God,

I want you to be my king. Thank you that I can trust you to lead me the right way. Please help me to do what you say, even when it is hard.

Amen.

Thinking about this week

What has been good?	What has been hard?
How have I been feeling?	What am I thankful for?
How have I followed Jesus?	Who can I thank?

Following Jesus: week 2

Date _____

> My answer would be that you can't show me
> your faith if you don't do anything.
> But I will show you my faith by the good I do.
> (James chapter 2 verse 18)

One part of being a Christian is believing in Jesus.
This happens in my mind and in my heart.

Another part of being a Christian is following Jesus.
This happens in the things I do.

Read James chapter 2 verses 14-18

Doing good things does not make God love me.
God already loves me! I do good things because I love him too.
I want to make him happy.

I show God I love him by trying to do what he wants.
This makes God happy. And it is good for me too!

When Jesus lived on earth, he always did what God wanted.
This is how I want to live too.
Following Jesus means trying to be like him.

The Holy Spirit helps me
to do what God wants.
He is changing my heart.
He is making me more like Jesus.

Following Jesus is not always easy.
But it is the best way to live!

1. How do you show God that you love him?

2. When is following Jesus hard for you?

Dear Lord Jesus,

Thank you that you always did what God wanted. I want to be more like you. Please help me to live the way you did.

Amen.

Thinking about this week

What has been good?	What has been hard?
How have I been feeling?	Do I need any help?
How have I followed Jesus?	Who can I ask for help?

Following Jesus: week 3

Date _____

> **We get our new life from the Spirit,
> so we should follow the Spirit.
> (Galatians chapter 5 verse 25)**

The Bible says that when I follow Jesus, I am like a strong tree that grows fruit.

The Holy Spirit grows a kind of fruit in my heart.
But this fruit is not apples or bananas!
It is things like love, peace and kindness.
These things make me more like Jesus.

Read Galatians chapter 5 verses 22-25

The Holy Spirit is growing good fruit in my heart.
He makes me strong inside so I can do what God wants.
The Holy Spirit helps me to make good choices.
He helps me show God's love to the people around me.

The Holy Spirit is making me more like Jesus.
But I am still me!
I am growing into the person
God made me to be.

I ask God to show me
how to live every day.
The Holy Spirit always helps me.
He always leads me the right way.

1. What kind of fruit is the Holy Spirit growing in your heart?

2. What help do you need from the Holy Spirit today?

Dear Holy Spirit,

Thank you that you are growing good fruit in my heart. Please keep making me more like Jesus. Please help me show God's love to the people around me.

Amen.

Thinking about this week

What has been good?	What has been hard?
How have I been feeling?	How have I been kind?
How have I followed Jesus?	Who has been kind to me?

Following Jesus: week 4

Date _____

> **Mary said, "I am the Lord's servant. Let this thing you have said happen to me!" Then the angel went away.**
>
> **(Luke chapter 1 verse 38)**

Mary was very young. She was going to get married soon.
She thought she would have a normal life.
But then something amazing happened.

Read Luke chapter 1 verses 26-38

God chose Mary to be Jesus's mother.
This was not what she had planned!
Mary did not know what would happen in the future.
But she knew that God was good.
She trusted God to be with her and help her.

Sometimes I feel worried about the future.
I feel afraid because I do not know what will happen.

But God knows what will happen. So following Jesus gives me peace. I can trust him to be with me and help me every day.

There are lots of things going on in my life.
Sometimes I forget to talk to Jesus.
Even when I forget Jesus,
he is still with me.

But when I ask Jesus for help,
he gives me his peace.
I know I need Jesus's
help every day.

1. How does trusting God help you when you feel worried?

2. How do you keep following Jesus when there are lots of things going on?

Dear Lord Jesus,

Thank you that you give me peace when I am afraid. Please help me to keep talking to you. Thank you that you are always with me.

Amen.

Thinking about this week

What has been good?	What has been hard?
How have I been feeling?	Is there anything I want to talk about?
How have I followed Jesus?	Who can I talk with?

Thinking about this topic

| What was this topic about? | What new things have I learned? |

| What has helped me? | Do I have any questions? |

| What did I like most? | Who can I ask? |

My prayer about following Jesus

Trusting God when life is hard

God knows that my life is hard sometimes.

It is okay to ask him questions.

It is okay to tell him how I really feel.

Trusting God when life is hard: week 1

Date _____

> Then the man said, "Your name will not be Jacob.
> Your name will now be Israel.
> I give you this name because you have fought
> with God and with men, and you have won."
>
> (Genesis chapter 32 verse 28)

Jacob had been away from home for a long time.
He prayed that his family would let him come home.

Then something strange happened.
God came and tried to beat Jacob in a fight!
This was called wrestling.

Read Genesis chapter 32 verses 22-28

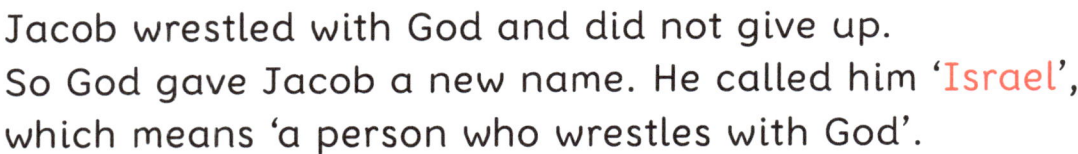

Jacob wrestled with God and did not give up.
So God gave Jacob a new name. He called him 'Israel',
which means 'a person who wrestles with God'.

Sometimes I am afraid to ask God questions or tell him how I feel. I think if I complain to God, it might make him angry.

But God wants me to wrestle with him like Jacob did.
This means I can tell him if I feel sad or angry.
I can ask him why he lets
bad things happen.
And I can complain to him
when life does not seem fair.

God wants me to be honest with him.
When I am honest with God,
it helps our friendship grow.

1. When life is hard, what do you want to say to God?

2. Why do you think God wants us to be honest with him?

Dear Father God,

Thank you that you want me to be honest with you. Please help me to tell you how I feel. Please help me when life is hard.

Amen.

Thinking about this week

What has been good?	What has been hard?
How have I been feeling?	What am I thankful for?
How have I been honest with God?	Who can I thank?

Trusting God when life is hard: week 2

Date _____

> **But Moses begged the LORD his God,
> "LORD, don't let your anger destroy your people…"
> So the LORD felt sorry for the people. He did not do what he said he might do—he did not destroy them.**
> **(Exodus chapter 32 verses 11 and 14)**

God was very angry with his people.
They had done something very bad.
God told their leader Moses that he was going to kill them.

Moses was very upset. He argued with God.
He asked God to change his mind.

Read Exodus chapter 32 verses 7-14

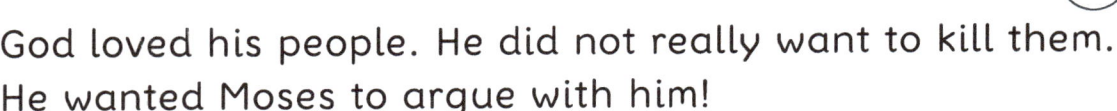

God loved his people. He did not really want to kill them.
He wanted Moses to argue with him!

When Moses argued, it showed that he knew what God was like.
And it showed that Moses loved the people as much as God did.
That made God happy. He did what Moses asked.
He forgave the people.

The Bible says that God is always good and loving.
But sometimes I do not understand what he does.
Being friends with God means
I can ask him questions.
I can even argue with him like Moses did.

God does not always answer my questions.
But he helps me to keep trusting him
when I am confused.

1. Do you ever feel confused about what God is doing?

2. What does the Bible say about what God is like?

Dear Father God,

Thank you that you are always good and loving. Thank you that I can ask you questions. Please help me keep trusting you when I am confused.

Amen.

Thinking about this week

| What has been good? | What has been hard? |

| How have I been feeling? | Do I need any help? |

| How have I been honest with God? | Who can I ask for help? |

Trusting God when life is hard: week 3

Date _____

> **After the LORD had finished talking to Job, he spoke to Eliphaz from Teman. He said, "I am angry with you and your two friends, because you did not tell the truth about me, as my servant Job did.**
>
> **(Job chapter 42 verse 7)**

Job was a good man. But lots of bad things happened to him. Job complained to God.
He said what had happened to him was not fair.

Job's friends thought God was punishing Job for doing something bad. But this was not true. God was angry with Job's friends because they were unkind to Job.

Read Job chapter 42 verses 1-7

Sometimes my life is very hard.
But I am afraid to complain to God.
I do not want to say something that is wrong. So I stay quiet.
I hide my thoughts and feelings.

When Job complained to God, he said some things that were wrong. But God forgave him.
God was happy that Job was honest with him.
He wants me to be honest with him too.

Sometimes my thoughts and feelings seem very wrong.
But God does not want me to hide them from him.
He can only help me if I am honest with him.

1. Do you ever hide your thoughts and feelings from God?

2. How can God help you when you are honest with him?

Dear Father God,

Thank you that you understand my thoughts and feelings. Please help me to be honest with you. Please forgive me when I say things that are wrong.

Amen.

Thinking about this week

What has been good?	What has been hard?
How have I been feeling?	How have I been kind?
How have I been honest with God?	Who has been kind to me?

Trusting God when life is hard: week 4

Date _____

> I begged the Lord three times to take this problem away from me. But the Lord said, "My grace is all you need. Only when you are weak can everything be done completely by my power."
>
> (2 Corinthians chapter 12 verses 8-9)

Paul told lots of people about Jesus. He started lots of churches. But there were some hard things in his life too.

In this letter Paul talked about something in his life that was hard. It hurt him and made him feel weak.
He asked God to take it away. But God said no.

Read 2 Corinthians chapter 12 verses 6-10

God wanted Paul to learn that he did not have to be strong. He only had to trust God. God was strong enough to help Paul do everything he needed to do.

I ask God for help, like Paul.
But sometimes God does not do what I want.
Sometimes he says no to me too.

When God says no,
I try to keep trusting him.
I do not always understand
why God says no.
But I know he loves me.
I know he knows best.
He is with me even
when life is hard.

1. Has God ever said no to something you really wanted?

2. How can you keep trusting God even when life is hard?

Dear Father God,

It is hard for me when you do not do what I want. Thank you that you know best. Please help me to keep trusting you.

Amen.

Thinking about this week

What has been good?	What has been hard?
How have I been feeling?	Is there anything I want to talk about?
How have I been honest with God?	Who can I talk with?

Thinking about this topic

What was this topic about?

What new things have I learned?

What has helped me?

Do I have any questions?

What did I like most?

Who can I ask?

My prayer about trusting God when life is hard

Winning the spiritual war

The Bible says there is a devil
who fights against God.
He hates everything good.
But Jesus has already won the spiritual war!

Winning the spiritual war: week 1

Date _____

> **Control yourselves and be careful!
> The devil is your enemy, and he goes around like a roaring lion looking for someone to attack and eat. Refuse to follow the devil. Stand strong in your faith.
> (1 Peter chapter 5 verses 8-9)**

Sometimes I wonder why bad things happen in the world. And I wonder why it is so hard for me to do what God wants.

The Bible says there is another world that I cannot see. It is the spiritual world where God lives. There is a war going on there. God is fighting against the devil.

Read 1 Peter chapter 5 verses 8-11

The devil hates everything that is good.
Sin and death come from him.
But God is much stronger than the devil.
So Father God sent Jesus to win the spiritual war.
Jesus died to save us from sin.
And he beat death by coming back to life!

The devil knows he has lost the spiritual war.
But he is still trying to pull people away from God.
And God is working hard to save people from the devil.

The war is still going on.
But I know that one day,
it will be over.
Jesus has already won!

1. How does it feel to know that Jesus has won the spiritual war?

2. What do you think the world will be like when the spiritual war is over?

Dear Lord Jesus,

Thank you that you have won the spiritual war. Thank you that you are stronger than the devil. Please help me to do what you want.

Amen.

Thinking about this week

What has been good?	What has been hard?
How have I been feeling?	What am I thankful for?
Where have I seen God's goodness?	Who can I thank?

Winning the spiritual war: week 2

Date _____

> [Jesus said to the Jewish leaders,] "Your father is the devil… There is no truth in him. He is like the lies he tells. Yes, the devil is a liar. He is the father of lies."
>
> (John chapter 8 verses 44)

Some important people did not believe what Jesus said. They wanted to kill him. Jesus said they were listening to lies that came from the devil.

Read John chapter 8 verses 39-44

The spiritual war is happening in the spiritual world.
But it is happening in my life too.
The devil wants to pull me away from God.

The devil puts lies in my mind.
He tries to make me believe things that are not true.

Sometimes he makes me believe that doing something bad will help me. That is not true. When I do bad things, it hurts me.

Sometimes he makes me believe
God has stopped loving me.
That is not true either!
God always loves me,
even when I do bad things.

God always tells the truth.
So I try to remember what
God says in the Bible.
This helps me know when
the devil is telling me lies.
I fight the devil's lies with God's truth.

1. What lies does the devil put in your mind?

2. What truths from the Bible can help you fight these lies?

Dear Father God,

Thank you that you always tell the truth. Please help me to fight the devil's lies with your truth.

Amen.

Thinking about this week

What has been good?	What has been hard?
How have I been feeling?	Do I need any help?
Where have I seen God's goodness?	Who can I ask for help?

Winning the spiritual war: week 3

Date _____

> **Depend on the Lord for your strength.
> Put your trust in his great power.
> Wear the full armour of God. Wear God's armour so that you can fight against the devil's clever tricks.
> (Ephesians chapter 6 verses 10-11)**

When someone fights in a war, they wear armour to keep their body safe. The things I need to fight the devil are like spiritual armour. They keep my heart and my mind safe.

Read Ephesians chapter 6 verses 10-18

First I need God's truth. This is like a belt.
It holds all the other things together. And I know that Jesus's goodness covers my heart to keep it safe.

I remember that Jesus has saved me from sin.
I remember that God has given me his grace.
This is like a helmet that keeps my mind safe.

Being God's friend gives me peace.
It is like a strong pair of shoes.

Following Jesus keeps me safe too.
It is like having a shield around me.

The Bible is like a sword.
I use truth from the Bible
to fight the devil's lies.

Whenever I am afraid, I pray.
God will always help me fight the devil's lies.

1. Which parts of your spiritual armour are strong? Which parts are not strong?

2. What help do you need from God today?

Dear Father God,

Thank you that you help me fight the devil's lies. Please help me to keep my spiritual armour strong.

Amen.

Thinking about this week

What has been good?	What has been hard?
How have I been feeling?	How have I been kind?
Where have I seen God's goodness?	Who has been kind to me?

Winning the spiritual war: week 4

Date _____

> But in all these troubles we have complete victory through God, who has shown his love for us.
> (Romans chapter 8 verse 37)

Sometimes thinking about the spiritual war makes me feel afraid.
But then I remember that God is much stronger than the devil.
And I remember that Jesus has already won the war.

The Bible says I do not need to be afraid of anything.
Nothing can take me away from God's love.

Read Romans chapter 8 verses 33-39

Bad things still happen in the world.
Sometimes my life will be hard.
But one day God will end the spiritual war.
He will make everything good again.
Then I will live with him forever.

Jesus has won the war.
That means I have won the war too!
I am friends with God.
He helps me fight the devil's lies.

Whatever happens,
I am always safe with Jesus.
As long as I stay close to Jesus,
I do not need to be afraid.

1. When you are afraid, what makes you feel better?

2. How does it feel to know that nothing can take you away from God's love?

Dear Lord Jesus,

Thank you that I am safe with you. Please help me not to be afraid. Please help me to stay close to you.

Amen.

Thinking about this week

| What has been good? | What has been hard? |

| How have I been feeling? | Is there anything I want to talk about? |

| Where have I seen God's goodness? | Who can I talk with? |

Thinking about this topic

What was this topic about?

What new things have I learned?

What has helped me?

Do I have any questions?

What did I like most?

Who can I ask?

My prayer about winning the spiritual war

Living forever with God

God has made a wonderful promise.

One day he will make everything good again.

Then I will live with him forever.

Living forever with God: week 1

Date _____

> **When this happens, the Scriptures will be made true: "Death is swallowed in victory."**
>
> **(1 Corinthians chapter 15 verse 54)**

There are lots of good things in my life. But there are bad things too. The world God made is broken because of sin and death.
But one day, there will be no more sin or death.
God will make everything good,
like it was in the beginning.

Read 1 Corinthians chapter 15 verses 51-57

People cannot fix the world. But God can! Father God sent Jesus to win the spiritual war. Jesus beat death and saved us from sin. Now we can be friends with God.

The Bible says that one day, Jesus is going to come back to earth. Then God will make a new world, where everything is good.
I will live there with him forever! That is God's wonderful promise.

When I think about God's wonderful promise, it gives me hope. It makes me happy even when life is hard.

I know that one day everything will be good.
I am looking forward to that day!

1. What do you think God's new world will be like?

2. How can thinking about God's new world give you hope?

Dear Father God,

Thank you for your wonderful promise. Thank you that you are going to make everything good. Please give me hope when life is hard.

Amen.

Thinking about this week

| What has been good? | What has been hard? |

| How have I been feeling? | What am I thankful for? |

| How has God's promise given me hope? | Who can I thank? |

Living forever with God: week 2

Date _____

> **Then I saw a new heaven and a new earth…**
> **The one who was sitting on the throne said,**
> **"Look, I am making everything new!"**
> **(Revelation chapter 21 verses 1 and 5)**

Some people wonder if there is another life after we die.
The Bible says there is!

God gave a vision to a man called John.
He showed John a wonderful new world.
God will make this world in the future.
After I die, I will live with him there forever.

Read Revelation chapter 21 verses 1-5

Some parts of John's vision were very strange.
It was hard for him to understand it all.

But John saw wonderful things too. He saw God living with us in his new world. He saw that there was no sadness or death
God was the king. Everything was good.

This is what God's new world will be like!
All the good things in my life
will be even better.
And there will be no
bad things ever again.

In God's new world,
I will be happy all the time.
I will meet God face to face!
And I will live with him forever.

1. How will your life be different in God's new world?

2. What will it be like to meet God face to face?

Dear Father God,

Thank you that one day I will meet you face to face. Please help me to look forward to your new world.

Amen.

Thinking about this week

What has been good?	What has been hard?
How have I been feeling?	Do I need any help?
How has God's promise given me hope?	Who can I ask for help?

Living forever with God: week 3

Date _____

> [The Christians sang to God,] "You made them to be a kingdom and to be priests for our God. And they will rule on the earth."
> (Revelation chapter 5 verse 10)

God says that I am his child.
That means I can talk to him and ask him for help.
And he has given me a special job to do!

In God's new world, Jesus will be in charge. Christians will be his helpers. We will look after the new world and enjoy it. This is what God made us to do!

Read Revelation chapter 5 verses 8-12

God's new world is not here yet.
But my special job starts in the world that is here now.

I follow Jesus every day. I do what God wants.
I try to be kind and help people.
And I ask God to do good things in the world.

All these things bring God's goodness into the place where I live.
This makes the world better!
It gets the world ready for the day when Jesus will be in charge.

It makes God happy when I do the special job he has given me.

1. What will it be like to help Jesus look after God's new world?

2. How can you bring God's goodness into the place where you live?

Dear Father God,

Thank you that I will help Jesus look after your new world. Please help me to bring your goodness into the place where I live.

Amen.

Thinking about this week

What has been good?	What has been hard?
How have I been feeling?	How have I been kind?
How has God's promise given me hope?	Who has been kind to me?

Living forever with God: week 4

Date _____

> **You were raised from death with Christ. So live for what is in heaven, where Christ is sitting at the right hand of God.**
> **(Colossians chapter 3 verse 1)**

I know that the life I have now will end one day.
So it gives me hope to think about God's wonderful promise.
After I die I will live with him forever!

Read Colossians chapter 3 verses 1-4

I feel happy when I think about God's new world.
My life there will never end!

When my life is good, I look forward to a future that will be even better. And when my life is hard, I look forward to the day when God will make everything good.

When I feel upset, I remember how much God loves me.
I remember what Jesus has done for me.
And I remember that the Holy Spirit is making me strong inside.
I do not need to be afraid of anything.

One day I will live forever in God's wonderful new world.
And while I am here on earth,
I know that Jesus will
always be with me.

1. When you are upset, what can you remember about God?

2. How does it help to know that Jesus will always be with you?

Dear Father God,

Thank you that my life in your new world will go on forever. Please help me to remember that Jesus is always with me.

Amen.

Thinking about this week

What has been good?	What has been hard?
How have I been feeling?	Is there anything I want to talk about?
How has God's promise given me hope?	Who can I talk with?

Thinking about this topic

What was this topic about?

What new things have I learned?

What has helped me?

Do I have any questions?

What did I like most?

Who can I ask?

My prayer about living forever with God

Keep Learning

You are done! Thank you for reading this book! I hope it has helped you get to know God better.

Here are some websites where you can keep learning about Jesus and the Bible.

Valley of Springs: **valleyofsprings.com/easyread**

This is my website. You can download free easy read Bible lessons and find out more about following Jesus.
You can join my email list to find out about new easy read projects.
You can also buy my first book *'Refresh'*.

Count Everyone In: **counteveryonein.org.uk**

On this website there are videos about the Bible.
You can also buy easy read Bible study booklets.

Inclusive Online Activities: **inclusiveonlineactivities.com**

Here you can join online sessions for adults with learning disabilities. There are free worship and Bible sessions.

Fenland Community Church: **fcc.uk.net**

Here you can download more easy read Bible lessons.

Simply the Gospel: **simplythegospel.com**

Here you can download helpful worksheets to help you pray and learn about Jesus.

About Jo

I have worked with disabled people for 18 years.
I was a support worker and then a music therapist.
Now I help to lead a church group for people with learning difficulties.

I live with my husband Dan and our cat Dillon.
I like singing and working in my garden.
I also really like jelly babies!

My website is **valleyofsprings.com**.

 You can follow me on Facebook at **facebook.com/valleyofsprings**

 You can follow me on Instagram at **instagram.com/valleyofsprings**

My book 'Refresh' follows the same structure as this book.
It is written for people who can read well.

You can buy signed copies of 'Refresh' at **valleyofsprings.com/store**

You can also get it from Amazon and all good bookshops.

Thanks

Thank you to everyone who helped me with my first book, '**Refresh**'.

Thank you to Rea Toyne, Michael Hobbs, Sarah Couchman, Cate Allen and Annette Stuart, Jill and Jennie Marsden, Jenny Edwards and everyone else who tried out this book. You really helped to make it better!

Thank you to my Mum for reading this book and giving me advice.

Thank you to Janet Eardley, Ivy Blair and everyone else who helped me tell people about this book.

Thank you to Bob Hext from Crossbow Education for letting me use the Aravis font in this book.

Thank you to Leah Jeffery for making this book look so good!

Thank you to all the people who helped me publish this book: Dave & Jo Taylor, Joanna Walker, Hilja Jeffery, Nick Jones, Jill Marsden, Matt McChlery, Alison Hughes, Lesley and Andrew Davies, Ian and Lorna Hancock, Claire Brookson, Gill Brazier, Sophie and Mark Rolph.

Thank you Dan for helping me to keep going.

Thank you Jesus for always being with me.

Word meanings

Bible

The Bible is very special. It is made up of lots of books. They were written by people who knew God very well.

The Holy Spirit gave thoughts and ideas to the people who wrote the Bible. He helped them to say what he wanted them to say.

So the Bible is a message to people from God.
It tells us what God is like and teaches us how to follow Jesus.

Christian

A Christian is someone who has decided to follow Jesus. Christians believe that Jesus saved us from sin.
And we try to live the way he lived.

Father God sends the Holy Spirit to live inside every Christian. The Holy Spirit helps us to do what God wants.

Christians still do bad things, but God always forgives us. He keeps making us more like Jesus.

Church

A church is a group of Christians
who worship God and follow Jesus together.

The building where a church meets together
is also sometimes called a church.

Cross

Jesus was killed by people who did not believe what he said.
They nailed him to a big wooden cross.
This was a horrible way to die.

Jesus chose to let these people kill him.
When he died, he took away the bad things we have done.
He saved us from sin.

Then Father God brought Jesus back to life!
When Jesus came back to life he beat death forever.

David

David was a famous king in the Bible. He loved God.
You can read about how God chose him to be King
in 1 Samuel chapter 16.

Devil

The Bible says there is a devil who fights against God.
The devil hates everything good.
Sin and death come from him.

But God is much stronger than the devil.
Father God sent Jesus to save us from sin and beat death.
Jesus has won the spiritual war against the devil.

One day God will end the spiritual war.
Then he will make everything good.

Father God

God has three parts: Father God, Jesus and the Holy Spirit.

Father God made the world. And he made people.
He is in charge of everything. He loves us very much.

Following Jesus

Anyone can decide to follow Jesus.
Followers of Jesus are called Christians.
We believe that Jesus saved us from sin.
And we try to live the way he lived.

The Holy Spirit comes to live inside every Christian.
The Holy Spirit helps us to do what God wants.

Christians still do bad things, but God always forgives us.
He keeps making us more like Jesus.

Forgiveness

God forgives us when we do bad things.
He tells us to forgive people who do bad things to us.
Forgiveness means giving our angry feelings to God.

Forgiveness does not mean the bad things people did to us were okay. And it does not mean we have to stay friends with people who hurt us.

Grace

We all do bad things sometimes.
Nobody can be good all the time.

Father God sent Jesus to save us from sin.
When he died he took away the bad things we have done.
Now we can be friends with God!

We did not work to save ourselves.
God saved us because he loves us.
This is his special gift of grace.

Heart

In the Bible, the heart is a place deep down inside every person. It is where we make choices and decide how to live. So it is the kind of person we are inside.

Heaven

Heaven is a place we cannot see. It is where God lives.

The Bible says that God will make a wonderful new world one day. Everything will be good in God's new world. We will live there with him forever!

Holy Spirit

God has three parts: Father God, Jesus and the Holy Spirit.

The Holy Spirit lives inside every Christian.
He helps us to do what God wants.
He makes us more like Jesus.

Hope

Life can be hard sometimes.
Hope means looking forward to a better future.
It helps us to keep going.

I know that Jesus is always with me.
And I know God will make everything good one day.
These things give me hope.

Jesus

God has three parts:
Father God, Jesus and the Holy Spirit.
Jesus came to earth as a baby.
He was both human and God!
He helped people and told them about God.
He was the only human who was always good.

Jesus died on the cross to take away the bad things we have done. He saved us from sin.
He did this because he loves us so much.

Jesus came back to life on the first Easter Sunday.
He beat sin and death forever.
Now Jesus is in heaven with Father God.

The Bible says Jesus will come back to earth one day.
Then God will make everything good.

Paul

Paul was a famous Christian in the Bible.
He told people about Jesus and started churches.
You can read about how God changed Paul's life in Acts chapter 9.

Peace

The Bible says that trusting God gives us peace.
Having peace means feeling safe deep down in our hearts.

We can feel safe because God is good and strong.
He is always with us.
When we feel worried we can ask God to give us peace.

Prayer

Prayer is talking to God. We can pray to God any time.
We can talk to him about anything.
We do not need to use special words.
We can pray out loud, or quietly in our minds.
God is always listening.

Psalm

Psalms is a book of songs.
People wrote these songs to worship God.
They sang on their own and all together, like we do in church. We do not know the tunes to these songs.
But we can make up our own!

Save

When someone is in trouble, they need someone to save them.
The Bible says that we were in trouble because of sin.
We could not stop doing bad things.
We could not beat sin on our own.

That is why Father God sent Jesus to save us.
When Jesus died, he saved us from sin.
And he beat sin forever!

Sin

There is something inside us that wants to do bad things.
This is called sin. It makes us turn away from God.
The Bible says that we cannot stop doing bad things.
Sin is stronger than we are.

But when Jesus died, he beat sin forever.
He took away all the bad things we have done.
Now we can be friends with God!

Spiritual war

There is a war going on in the spiritual world.
It is a war between God and the devil.
The devil hates everything good.
He wants to pull people away from God.

Father God sent Jesus to win the spiritual war.
When Jesus came back to life,
he won the war against the devil.

One day God will end the spiritual war.
Then he will make everything good.

Spiritual world

The spiritual world is where God lives. We cannot see it.
The Bible says God is a spirit.
This means he does not have a body like us.
That is why we cannot see God.
But even though we cannot see him, he is always with us.

Trusting God

Trusting God means believing what the Bible says about him. The Bible says that God is good and always does good things. The Bible says God loves us and always tells the truth.

Believing these things about God gives us hope.
It helps us to keep following Jesus when life is hard.

Vision

A vision is like a dream that someone has while they are awake. In the Bible, God sometimes gave people visions.
He showed them what was happening in the spiritual world.

Worship

Worship is anything we do that shows God we love him.
At church we sing songs to worship God.
But we can worship him in other ways too.
When we live in a way that makes God happy, that is worship. So we can worship God in all the things we do!

Wrestling

Wrestling is a type of fighting.
When people wrestle, they hold onto each other.
They try to pull the other person down to the ground.
They do not let go until they have won the fight.

Wrestling is a picture of our friendship with God.
God wants us to hold onto him and not let go.
He wants us to be honest with him.
He wants us tell him how we really feel.